Courage To Commit : 30 Days of Faith in Action

For permission requests, write to:
THE LIVING WORD JOURNEY
info@thelivingwordjourney.com
TheLivingWordJourney.com

First Edition

TABLE OF CONTENTS

WELCOME *to*
the COURAGE TO COMMIT 30 DAY CHALLENGE

This challenge was created with the heart and purpose of helping you grow deeper in your faith, strengthen your spiritual walk, and take purposeful action in your daily life. Not just about gaining knowledge, but about applying the wisdom and principles from the Bible to every aspect of your life. It is designed to guide you as you set intentional spiritual goals, with practical steps to help you grow in your relationship with God and actively live out His calling for your life.

We live in a world filled with distractions, and it can be easy to lose focus on our ultimate purpose. But as Christians, we are called to more than just exist; we are called to make an impact, to share the good news of Jesus Christ, and to be living examples of His love and grace. This workbook will encourage you to align your daily actions with God's will, to be disciplined in your study of Scripture, and to take meaningful steps toward fulfilling the mission God has given you.

Our Purpose as Christians

The Bible is clear about our purpose as believers: we are called to love God, love others, and go into the world to spread His message. Jesus commands us in Matthew 28:19-20, "Go therefore and make disciples of all nations, baptizing them in the name of the Father and of the Son and of the Holy Spirit, teaching them to observe all that I have commanded you." This is the Great Commission—our calling to share the Gospel and live as examples of God's love and truth.

In Acts 1:8, Jesus further reminds us: "But you will receive power when the Holy Spirit has come upon you, and you will be my witnesses in Jerusalem and in all Judea and Samaria, and to the end of the earth." The Holy Spirit equips us to live out this mission, empowering us to fulfill our purpose as His witnesses, wherever we are.

As you work through this workbook, keep in mind that each challenge and study is meant to help you grow not only in your understanding of God's Word but in your ability to take action. We are called to be doers of the Word, not just hearers (James 1:22). Every day is an opportunity to take one more step toward becoming the person God has called you to be, and to share His love with the world around you.

How to Use This Workbook

Welcome to the Courage to Commit 30-Day Challenge! This workbook is designed to guide you on a journey of spiritual growth and commitment through intentional reflection, scripture study, and daily action. Here's how to make the most of this resource:

Daily Structure

Each day combines three key elements to help you deepen your walk with God:

- Scripture: Start your day by reading and meditating on the scripture provided. Let the Word guide your thoughts and set the tone for the day.
- Reflection: Use the journaling sheets to center your thoughts. Write down your responses to the scripture, moments of conviction, or insights you gain as you dig deeper into what God is revealing to you.
- Daily Challenge : Take actionable steps to confront areas in your life that need growth or alignment with God's will. These challenges are practical and designed to help you live out your faith intentionally.

Journaling: A Key to Growth

The journaling pages are a tool for self-discovery and spiritual alignment. Here's how they can help you:

- Center Your Thoughts: Writing things down can bring clarity and focus, allowing you to organize your reflections and pinpoint what God is teaching you.
- Go Deeper: Journaling gives you space to explore questions like, "What is God asking of me?" or "How can I obey Him more fully?"
- Track Your Progress: By the end of the 30 days, you'll have a written record of how far you've come spiritually and where God has moved in your life.

Tips for Success

- Set Aside Time: Choose a consistent time each day to work through the challenge. Mornings or evenings often work well for focused reflection.
- Be Honest: This journey is between you and God. Write honestly and openly in your journaling sheets, even if the truths you confront are hard to face.
- Pray First: Begin each day with a prayer, asking God to open your heart and mind to His will.

By the end of this challenge, you'll have spent 30 days intentionally growing in faith, obedience, and courage to commit fully to God's call.

Week 1

SELF-EXAMINATION & REPENTANCE

Identify and confess sins, idols, and disobedience.

DAY 1

PRAY FOR CLARITY

Psalm 139:23-24

"Search me, God, and know my heart; test me and know my anxious thoughts. See if there is any offensive way in me, and lead me in the way everlasting."

Prayer Focus: Invite God to search your heart and reveal areas where idols or misplaced priorities exist.

Matthew 6:33

"But seek first his kingdom and his righteousness, and all these things will be given to you as well."

Prayer Focus:Pray for a heart that prioritizes God's kingdom and righteousness over worldly concerns.

Isaiah 44:9

"All who make idols are nothing, and the things they treasure are worthless."

Ask God to reveal hidden sins and idols in your life.

daily challenge

INVENTORY YOUR HEART

Colossians 3:2

"Set your minds on things above, not on earthly things."

Prayer focus: Ask for clarity in distinguishing between heavenly priorities and distractions rooted in earthly desires.

Matthew 6:19-21

"Do not store up for yourselves treasures on earth, where moths and vermin destroy, and where thieves break in and steal. But store up for yourselves treasures in heaven. For where your treasure is, there your heart will be also."

Prayer focus: Pray for insight into what treasures you might be holding onto that shift your focus away from God.

Reflect on where your time, energy, and finances are going. Identify anything you prioritize over God.

daily challenge

DAY 3

CONFESS & REPENT

1 John 1:9

"If we confess our sins, he is faithful and just and will forgive us our sins and purify us from all unrighteousness."

Write a letter to God confessing your sins and idols.

daily challenge

DAY 4

ADDRESS TOXIC WORDS

Proverbs 18:21

"Those who love to talk will experience the consequences, for the tongue can kill or nourish life."

Often, we unintentionally use words that hurt others or even ourselves. Complaints, sarcasm, gossip, or quick criticisms can easily slip into our daily conversations without us giving them much thought. These small, seemingly harmless comments can build up and have a negative impact sowing seeds of negativity in our own hearts. By becoming more mindful of our words and intentionally choosing to speak life, we can shift the atmosphere and encourage others, reflecting God's love and grace in every conversation.

Reflect on your recent words, identify areas of gossip or negativity, and commit to speaking life.

daily challenge

EXAMINE YOUR THOUGHTS

Philippians 4:6-7

"Do not be anxious about anything, but in every situation, by prayer and petition, with thanksgiving, present your requests to God. And the peace of God, which transcends all understanding, will guard your hearts and your minds in Christ Jesus."

Prayer focus: Present your need for clarity and trust in God's peace to guard your heart and mind.

Philippians 4:8

"And now dear brothers and sisters, let me say one more things as I close this letter. Fix your thoughts on what is true and honorable and right. Think about things that are pure and lovely and admirable. Think about things that are excellent and worthy of praise.

Write down recurring thoughts and evaluate them against Scripture.

daily challenge

DAY
6

IDENTIFY WHAT YOU'RE AVOIDING

James 1:22

"Do not merely listen to the word, and so deceive yourselves. Do what it says."

Many people twist or selectively interpret Scripture to justify their actions, avoiding the full conviction of God's Word. True obedience requires not just hearing God's commands but actively living them out, even when it challenges our personal desires or sinful habits.

Think about where you've been avoiding obedience to God and take one step today to start following Him in that area.

DAY 7

WORSHIP ONLY GOD

Exodus 20:3

"Do not worship any other Gods beside me."

The Bible teaches that people can worship other gods or things through idolatry, prioritizing material possessions, self-worship, or false teachings over God. Jesus warns against serving money and seeking personal pleasures or power as substitutes for devotion to Him. Ultimately, anything that takes God's rightful place in our hearts—whether it's wealth, self-interest, or worldly success—becomes an idol and a form of misplaced worship.

Remove physical or digital distractions that have become idols.

daily challenge

Weekly Recap

- What stood out to you in the scriptures and challenges this week?
- How did God speak to you through the daily tasks?

Week 2

IDOLS & SACRIFICE

Recognize and release idols, making room for God.

FAST FROM A COMFORT

Matthew 6:16-18

And when you fast, don't make it obvious, as the hypocrites do, who try to look pale and disheveled so people will admire them for their fasting. I assure you, that is the only reward they will ever get. 17.But when you fast, comb your hair and wash your face. 18. Then no one will suspect you are fasting, except your Father, who knows what you do in Secret. And your farther, who knows all secrets, will reward you.

Choose one comfort to give up this week and replace it with prayer or Bible reading.

daily challenge

_____
_____
_____
_____
_____
_____
_____
_____
_____
_____
_____
_____
_____
_____
_____
_____
_____
_____

DAY
9

EVALUATE YOUR RELATIONSHIPS

1 Corinthians 15:33

"Do not be misled: 'Bad company corrupts good character'"

Proverbs 13:20:

"Walk with the wise and become wise, for a companion of fools suffers harm."

God wants us to walk with the wise because wise people seek His guidance, live according to His truth, and help us grow in our faith and understanding. By surrounding ourselves with wise believers, we are more likely to make godly choices, avoid pitfalls, and deepen our relationship with God.

Reflect on whether any relationships take God's place in your life. Pray for wisdom to set boundaries.

daily challenge

DAY 10 SURRENDER CONTROL

Proverbs 3:5-6

Trust in the Lord with all your heart; do not depend on your own understanding. Seek his will in all you do, and he will direct your paths.

Philippians 4:6-7

Do not be anxious about anything, but in every situation, by prayer and petition, with thanksgiving, present your requests to God

One way a person can actively work toward surrendering control and trusting God is through consistent prayer and meditation on His Word. By setting aside time each day to seek God's will, ask for His guidance, and release personal anxieties, a person can gradually learn to trust God's plan over their own. This act of surrender allows God's peace to replace fear and uncertainty.

Write down what you're holding onto tightly and surrender it to God in prayer.

daily challenge

DAY
11

SACRIFICE YOUR SCHEDULE

Isaiah 26:3:

Peace comes from keeping focused on God

Dedicate extra time to God today
through Scripture reading, prayer,
or worship.

daily challenge

EXAMINE MATERIALISM

Matthew 6:19-21

19 "Don't store up treasures here on earth, where moths eat them and rust destroys them, and where thieves break in and steal. 20 Store your treasures in heaven, where moths and rust cannot destroy, and thieves do not break in and steal. 21 Wherever your treasure is, there the desires of your heart will also be.

Write a list of possessions you treasure most and ask God to help you detach your heart from earthly things.

DAY 13

GIVE GENEROUSLY

Deuteronomy 15:10

"You shall give to him freely, and your heart shall not be grudging when you give to him, because for this the Lord your God will bless you in all your work and in all that you undertake"

Luke 6:38

"Give, and it will be given to you; good measure, pressed down, and shaken together, and running over, shall men give into your bosom"

Choose something to give away and reflect on how this shifts your focus from self to others.

daily challenge

DAY
14

REST IN GOD ALONE

Matthew 11:28-30

"Come to me, all who labor and are heavy laden, and I will give you rest" 29. "Take my yoke upon you, and learn from me; for I am gentle and lowly in heart, and you will find rest for your souls" 30. "For my yoke is easy, and my burden is light"

Practice a Sabbath by disconnecting from work or productivity and focusing on rest in God.

daily challenge

Weekly Recap

- What areas of obedience did you notice improvement?
- Where do you feel you still need to grow?

Week 3

RENEW YOUR MIND

Transform thoughts and words to reflect God's truth.

DAY
15
MEMORIZE SCRIPTURE

Acts 3:9

"Repent, then, and turn back, so that your sins may be wiped away, that times of refreshing may come from the presence of the Lord.". This verse emphasizes the importance of turning away from sin and turning towards God to receive forgiveness.

God wants us to memorize Scripture because it strengthens our faith, helps us resist temptation, and provides guidance in times of need. As Jesus demonstrated in Matthew 4:4, when He was tempted by Satan, He responded with Scripture, showing us how essential God's Word is in spiritual battles. Memorizing Scripture allows us to internalize His truth, making it readily available to shape our thoughts, actions, and decisions, and to align our lives with His will.

Choose a verse that counters a recurring sinful thought and commit it to memory.

daily challenge

_____

_____

_____

_____

_____

_____

_____

_____

_____

_____

_____

_____

_____

_____

DAY 16

PRACTICE GRATITUDE

1 Thessalonians 5:16-18:

"Rejoice always, pray continually, give thanks in all circumstances; for this is God's will for you in Christ Jesus"

Psalm 118:29:

"Give thanks to the LORD, for he is good; his love endures forever"

The Bible teaches that a person can practice gratitude through consistent thanksgiving, worship, and recognizing God's goodness in all circumstances. Practicing gratitude involves acknowledging God's blessings in every situation, from the smallest to the most challenging, and offering praise through prayer and worship

Write down 10 blessings and commit to thanking God daily this week.

daily challenge

DAY 17

GUARD YOUR TONGUE

James 1:19-20

19 My dear brothers and sisters, take note of this: Everyone should be quick to listen, slow to speak and slow to become angry, 20 because human anger does not produce the righteousness that God desires.

Remember there is power in the tongue so be mindful about the words you use.

Practice silence for an hour and reflect on speaking with intention.

daily challenge

DAY 18

FILTER YOUR INPUT

Ephesians 6:11 "Put on the full armor of God, so that you can take your stand against the devil's schemes.".

Proverbs 4:23: "Above all else, guard your heart, for everything you do flows from it."

1 Thessalonians 5:22: "Abstain from every form of evil."

James 4:7: "Submit yourselves, then, to God. Resist the devil, and he will flee from you."

We should limit exposure to ungodly media and negative conversations that can distract us from recognizing God's blessings. Instead, we can replace these with worship, focusing on praising God and reflecting on his goodness in every circumstance.

Limit exposure to unholy media or
conversations and replace them
with worship or sermons.

daily challenge

ENCOURAGE OTHERS

Hebrews 10:24-25

"And let us consider how to stir up one another to love and good works, not neglecting to meet together, as is the habit of some, but encouraging one another, and all the more as you see the Day drawing near"

1 Thessalonians 5:11

"Therefore encourage one another and build one another up, just as you are doing"

Speak life into someone by sending an uplifting message or praying for them.

daily challenge

DAY
20

DECLARE SCRIPTURE OVER YOUR LIFE

Romans 12:2

"Do not conform to the pattern of this world, but be transformed by the renewing of your mind.

Romans 10:9

If you declare with your mouth, 'Jesus is Lord,' and believe in your heart that God raised him from the dead, you will be saved.

Declaring Scripture over your life involves speaking God's Word aloud and applying it to your circumstances, faith, and desires. By regularly meditating on verses that align with God's promises and truth, you can declare them with conviction, such as claiming verses of healing, peace, or provision, and allowing them to shape your mindset and actions. This practice affirms God's authority in your life and strengthens your faith in His ability to fulfill His promises.

Affirm transformation by speaking this verse aloud in prayer.

daily challenge

_____

_____

_____

_____

_____

_____

_____

_____

_____

_____

_____

_____

_____

_____

_____

_____

JOURNAL YOUR PROGRESS

DAY
21

2 Corinthians 5:17

"Therefore, if anyone is in Christ, he is a new creation. The old has passed away; behold, the new has come.".

Reflect on changes in your heart, thoughts, and words throughout the challenge.

daily challenge

Weekly Recap

- What actions or commitments do you feel called to make moving forward?
- How will you apply what you've learned in the coming week?

daily challenge

Week 4

LIVING SACRIFICE

Commit fully to God's purposes with boldness and love.

DAY 22

SUBMIT YOUR WHOLE SELF

Romans 12:1

Therefore, I urge you, brothers and sisters, in view of God's mercy, to offer your bodies as a living sacrifice, holy and pleasing to God—this is your true and proper worship.

Lord, I offer myself to You today as a living sacrifice—my body, my mind, and my soul. I surrender all that I am, asking You to transform me by the renewing of my mind. Help me to live according to Your will, to seek what is good, pleasing, and perfect in Your eyes. Guide me to honor You in every thought, word, and action. In Jesus' name, Amen.

Pray to offer your body, mind, and soul as a living sacrifice.

daily challenge

SERVE OTHERS

Mark 10:45

For even the Son of Man did not come to be served, but to serve, and to give his life as a ransom for many."

According to the Bible, Jesus served others in numerous profound ways, exemplifying selflessness, compassion, and humility. Here are a few key ways He served:

1. **Healing the Sick and Performing Miracles.** Jesus healed the blind, deaf, and sick, showing compassion for those in physical need. In Matthew 14:14, *"When Jesus landed and saw a large crowd, he had compassion on them and healed their sick.

2. **Washing His Disciples' Feet** In John 13:12-15, Jesus humbly washed His disciples' feet, demonstrating that true leadership comes through serving others, regardless of their status. "I have set you an example that you should do as I have done for you."

3. **Feeding the Hungry:** Jesus fed thousands of people who were physically hungry, providing not just spiritual nourishment but also meeting their immediate needs. In John 6:35, He says, *"I am the bread of life. Whoever comes to me will never go hungry."

4. **Teaching and Guiding:** Jesus served by teaching others about the Kingdom of God, offering wisdom, parables, and guidance on how to live according to God's will. In Matthew 5-7, the Sermon on the Mount, He taught His followers about love, mercy, and righteousness.

5. **Forgiving Sins:** One of the greatest acts of service was Jesus' willingness to forgive sins, showing His deep love and desire for people to be reconciled with God. In Mark 2:5, when He saw the faith of a paralyzed man's friends, He said, *"Son, your sins are forgiven."*

6. **Sacrificing His Life:** Ultimately, Jesus served humanity through His sacrificial death on the cross for the forgiveness of sins. John 15:13 highlights this ultimate act of love: *"Greater love has no one than this: to lay down one's life for one's friends."*

Through His actions and teachings, Jesus perfectly modeled the way believers are called to serve others, with humility, love, and a willingness to put others' needs before our own.

Serve someone today, reflecting Jesus' example of humility and love.

daily challenge

DAY 24

SHARE YOUR FAITH

John 8:17-18

"In your own Law it is written that the testimony of two witnesses is true. I am one who testifies for myself; my other witness is the Father, who sent me".

2 Corinthians 3:2-3

"You yourselves are our letter of recommendation, written on our hearts, to one known and read by all".

Share how Jesus is transforming you with someone who doesn't believe.

daily challenge

DAY
25

PRAY BOLDLY

2 Timothy 1:7
The Holy Spirit gives us power, love, and self-discipline to lead with boldness.

Proverbs 28:1
The righteous are bold because they know that God is for them and what they have to say is important.

Praying boldly means approaching God with confidence, faith, and trust in His ability to answer. As Hebrews 4:16 reminds us, we can come boldly before God's throne, knowing He hears our prayers when they align with His will (1 John 5:14-15). Bold prayer also involves persistent asking (Luke 18:1-8) and speaking with authority, trusting that nothing is impossible with God (Matthew 17:20).

Pray for boldness to follow Jesus, even in sacrifice.

daily challenge

_____
_____
_____
_____
_____
_____
_____
_____
_____
_____
_____
_____
_____
_____
_____

DAY
26

RECONNECT WITH A HARD RELATIONSHIP

Matthew 5:44

"But I say to you, love your enemies, bless those who curse you, do good to those who hate you, and pray for those who spitefully use you and persecute you".

Extend forgiveness or love to someone you've struggled with.

daily challenge

COMMIT TO
DISCIPLESHIP

Matthew 28:19-20

19 Therefore go and make disciples of all nations, baptizing them in the name of the Father and of the Son and of the Holy Spirit, 20 and teaching them to obey everything I have commanded you. And surely I am with you always, to the very end of the age."

Commit to leading or supporting others in their walk with Christ.

daily challenge

_____

_____

_____

_____

_____

_____

_____

_____

_____

_____

_____

_____

_____

_____

DAY
28

CELEBRATE SMALL WINS

Philippians 1:6: "I'm sure about this: the one who started a good work in you will stay with you to complete the job by the day of Christ Jesus".

Philippians 4:4: "Rejoice in the Lord always. I will say it again: Rejoice!".

Thank God for progress in identifying
and letting go of idols.

daily challenge

DAY
29

PUBLIC DECLARATION

Matthew 10:32: "Those who declare publicly that they belong to me, I will do the same for them before my Father in heaven".

Romans 10:9-14: "If you openly declare that Jesus is Lord and believe in your heart that God raised him from the dead, you will be saved".

Share your journey with a group or online to inspire others.

daily challenge

_____
_____
_____
_____
_____
_____
_____
_____
_____
_____
_____
_____
_____
_____
_____
_____

DAY
30

REAFFIRM YOUR COMMITMENT

Romans 12:2 ESV

Do not be conformed to this world, but be transformed by the renewal of your mind, that by testing you may discern what is the will of God, what is good and acceptable and perfect.

1 John 3:4 ESV

Everyone who makes a practice of sinning also practices lawlessness; sin is lawlessness.

A person can reaffirm their commitment to God through prayer, repentance, and intentional acts of worship. This includes seeking God in prayer, expressing gratitude, and asking for His guidance to stay faithful. Additionally, reflecting on Scripture, renewing one's focus on God's purpose, and making intentional choices to live according to His will, such as serving others and following His commands, are ways to strengthen that commitment. As Romans 12:1-2 encourages, offering yourself as a living sacrifice is a continual act of reaffirming your devotion to God.

Page 68

Re-read your confessions and progress, and pray to stay aligned with God moving forward.

daily challenge

_____
_____
_____
_____
_____
_____
_____
_____
_____
_____
_____
_____
_____
_____
_____
_____
_____
_____
_____

Congratulations!

You've completed the 30-day challenge, and we commend you for your commitment to growing in your faith and deepening your relationship with God. This is a significant achievement, and your dedication to studying the Bible, reflecting on its teachings, and taking action each day has set you on a powerful path of spiritual growth.

As you reflect on the past 30 days, take a moment to celebrate how far you've come. Whether you feel that you've made great strides or have only begun to scratch the surface, remember that every step you take in faith is a victory. The journey of growth and transformation doesn't end here—it's a lifelong process. And you've made an important investment in that process!

Keep Going: Revisit and Stay Mindful
The journey of spiritual growth is ongoing. Don't hesitate to revisit this challenge periodically to refresh your commitment, re-align your goals, and keep yourself focused on the actions that will help you continue growing in faith. Just as our relationship with God requires daily attention, so too does our spiritual discipline. Repeating this challenge will reinforce the habits and principles you've started, allowing you to grow even deeper in your walk with God.

Try Another Challenge!

7-DAY HEALING FOR THE BETRAYED

"A short but powerful journey for the betrayed seeking healing, clarity, and renewal.

OVERCOMING DEPRESSION

Explore the root causes of depression and get faith-based solutions, scripture breakdowns, and practical steps for healing, renewal, and lasting transformation..

I KNOW WHO I AM

In a world filled with noise and confusion, knowing who you are in Christ is your greatest strength.

🌐 WEBSITE
TheLivingWordJourney.com